VICTORIAN LIFE

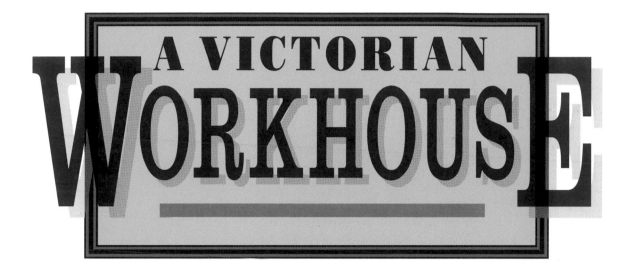

A VICTORIAN
WORKHOUSE

JOHN BARWELL

Wayland

VICTORIAN LIFE

A VICTORIAN CHRISTMAS

A VICTORIAN FACTORY

A VICTORIAN HOLIDAY

A VICTORIAN HOSPITAL

A VICTORIAN KITCHEN

A VICTORIAN SCHOOL

A VICTORIAN STREET

A VICTORIAN SUNDAY

A VICTORIAN WORKHOUSE

VICTORIAN CLOTHES

VICTORIAN TOYS AND GAMES

VICTORIAN TRANSPORT

HOW WE LEARN ABOUT THE VICTORIANS

Queen Victoria reigned from 1837 to 1901, a time when Britain went through enormous social and industrial changes. We can learn about Victorians in various ways. We can still see many of their buildings standing today, we can look at their documents, maps and artefacts – many of which can be found in museums. Photography, invented during Victoria's reign, gives us a good picture of life in Victorian Britain. In this book you will see what Victorian life was like through some of this historical evidence.

Series design: Pardoe Blacker Ltd
Editor: Sarah Doughty

First published in 1994 by Wayland (Publishers) Ltd,
61 Western Road, Hove, East Sussex BN3 1JD, England

© Copyright 1994 Wayland (Publishers) Ltd

British Library Cataloguing in Publication Data
Barwell, John.
 Victorian Workhouse (Victorian Life Series)
 I. Title II. Series
 362.50941

ISBN 0 7502 1158 X

Printed and bound in Great Britain by B.P.C.C Paulton Books Ltd

Cover picture: St James's Parish workhouse, London.

Picture acknowledgements:
John Barwell 9 (top); Bridgeman Art Library *cover*, 11 (top); Communist Party Library, Picture Library & Archive 21 (bottom), 22; E.T Archive 11 (bottom); Mary Evans Picture Library 6 (bottom), 7, 8, 9 (bottom), 10, 13 (bottom), 15, 16, 18, 19 (both), 20, 21 (top), 23 (bottom), 25 (top), 26, 27 (top); Glasgow City Libraries 5 (bottom), 6 (top); Hulton-Deutsch Collection 5 (top), 12, 14, 23 (top), 24, 25 (bottom); Mansell Collection 4; Norfolk Museums Service (Rural Life Museum, Gressenhall) 17 (top, middle), 27 (bottom); Wayland Picture Library 13 (top).

Thanks to Norfolk Museums Service for supplying items for use on pages 14 (bottom), 17 (bottom). Commissioned photography by G.G.S Photo Graphics.

CONTENTS

HARDSHIP AND THE POOR

What happens to people who cannot find work today? In Britain, those that are without a job are given money by the government to help them provide for themselves and their families. In Victorian times, however, there was no unemployment or sickness pay and there were no old age pensions. Families without money would expect to starve. In the nineteenth century, Britain was one of the richest countries in the world but also had many people who were very poor.

PRIVATE CHARITY

Even people in work found it difficult to make ends meet. Wages were low in Victorian Britain. This meant that many families could not afford to pay for the homes they rented. Cities were growing quickly and it was impossible to build enough homes to house everyone. A family often shared one room. The walls were usually damp and crumbling and few houses had running water. If the wage-earner of the family fell ill, the family had no money. The rich were sometimes willing to help by giving charity. They might, for example, bring a food basket. Most poor families, though, did not get this sort of help.

A lady brings help to a poor family.

THE POOREST WORKERS

Many of the poorest people were farm workers. They were paid very little, but they dared not complain as they might lose their jobs. Everyone in the family, including the children, had to work. Life was very hard for them. They rarely ate meat and lived mostly on bread and vegetables. Sometimes, a hungry labourer broke the law by poaching a rabbit, pigeon or pheasant from the private land of a rich neighbour. If the poacher was caught, he would be severely punished.

A young farm worker and his family.

WIDESPREAD HARDSHIP

Some of the paintings at this time did not show the hardship and suffering of ordinary country people. Look at this painting by Edwin Landseer (1802-73). It shows a poor drover along with his family from the Scottish Highlands, leaving their home and taking with them their herd of cows. The animals are going to be driven to the Lowlands, to cattle buyers in the south.

Paintings like these were very popular in Victorian times because they are like attractive postcards. The artist, Landseer, first visited Scotland in 1824. His picture of life in the Highlands does not give a full picture of what was happening at the time.

Edwin Landseer's *Highland Drover*.

HIGHLAND CLEARANCES

Hundreds of families in Scotland were being driven from the land and forced into cities or even abroad. Landowners found that a great deal of money could be made from sheep farming to provide mutton. Large flocks of sheep only needed a few men to look after them. The land was cleared of people to make way for sheep. Families were evicted, or forced to leave the homes they rented. Often their cottages were then burnt down. Many people were left homeless and penniless in this way.

A Scottish family forced to leave their cottage, 1854.

EVICTION

Eviction was the great fear of poor people everywhere. For many farm workers, the cottage was tied. That meant that if the workers lost their jobs, they also lost their homes. New ways of farming, and new machines, meant that fewer people were needed on the land, so many labourers lost their jobs. This picture shows a husband and his wife in Ireland pleading for their home. Other men are already beginning to destroy the roof of their house. Those who refused to leave their homes were dragged from them.

A couple plead for their home, 1848.

A violent demonstration against the Corn Laws, 1815.

BREAD RIOTS

Food was a main concern of the poor. Many poor people could not afford to buy bread. Grain was costly and this made the price of a loaf expensive. The Corn Laws of 1815 had stopped cheap foreign grain coming into Britain. The poor did not take kindly to the Corn Laws as they just added to the hardship they already faced. There were bread riots in London in 1815. People protested, sometimes violently, against the Corn Laws but this did not do any good. The Corn Laws were still in force when Victoria became Queen in 1837. Many people were finding it more and more difficult to manage.

THE OLD POOR LAW

If a family became too poor to keep themselves alive, they became paupers. As early as 1601, during the reign of Queen Elizabeth I, a Poor Law was passed which gave money from the parish to the poor, paid for by taxes. Until 1834, several years before Victoria came to the throne, each village or parish was supposed to look after its poor. The better-off had to pay a tax called the Poor Rate to help the paupers. The person in charge of collecting the money was called the Overseer of the Poor.

INDOOR AND OUTDOOR RELIEF

Pauper apprentices.

Since the seventeenth century, some parishes had built poorhouses. These were also called workhouses. They gave food and shelter to the poor. This kind of help was called 'indoor relief'. The workhouses were squalid and crowded but families could remain together. In other parishes, paupers were given a small sum of money, and perhaps food, each week, but stayed in their own homes. This was called 'outdoor relief'.

Work was sometimes found for poor children. A sum of up to £10 was offered to anyone who would take a child off the parish's hands. The children then became apprentices to the master. In return, the master looked after them until they were grown up. Such children were often badly treated.

THE HOUSE OF INDUSTRY

Sometimes the government gave permission for very big workhouses to be built. At first, these were called Houses of Industry. One of these workhouses was built at Gressenhall in Norfolk in 1777. It gave shelter to the poor from a number of parishes in the area. It looked like a stately home from the outside. Life inside though, was not pleasant for those who had to go there for help. It had become a great deal more unpleasant by the time Victoria became queen.

The Norfolk Rural Life Museum, formerly the workhouse at Gressenhall in Norfolk.

GROWING UNREST

Rick burners in Kent in 1830.

There was growing unrest in Britain long before Victoria came to the throne as people with jobs often could not afford to buy enough food. At Speenhamland in Berkshire in 1795 a new way of helping the poor was started and soon spread to the whole country. It was decided that the wages of farm labourers could be increased out of the poor rates.

But the labourers were angry about being treated as if they were paupers living on charity. They showed their anger in 1830. They set fire to ricks and barns and destroyed farm machiney. They hoped this action would persuade their employers not to replace them with labour-saving machines that might result in them losing their jobs.

GROWING DESPAIR

What does the picture tell us about the rick burner? He is a poor man with few possessions. His wife looks ill. He has four hungry children and an empty food cupboard. He is probably angry about his poor wages – and he might also be worried about the new threshing machines which could put him out of work. He would then have no choice but to go to the workhouse. A ghostly figure in the background seems to be urging him on to set fire to some more ricks.

The home of the rick burner.

THE OVERSEER OF THE POOR

Arriving at the workhouse.

Life was very hard, then, even for many in work. They would have to go to the Overseer of the Poor and ask him to make up their wages out of the money collected from the parish. Paupers were often made to feel ashamed of being 'on the parish'. It was even harder for those out of work. To get help, they might have to enter a workhouse. The better-off did not like paying the extra poor rate that was needed for this.

THE 'UNREFORMED' WORKHOUSE

Around the country, different parishes had different ways of giving help to poor people. In some parishes, only outdoor relief was given. However, some people felt that too many able-bodied people were getting this kind of help. Other villages built poorhouses. These were often miserable and overcrowded places. Parishes sometimes grouped together to build larger workhouses. Some workhouses, like St James's Workhouse in London, were thought to be too spacious and comfortable. Many felt that the Poor Law should be changed, and existing workhouses reformed.

St James's Workhouse, London, before 1834.

THE NEW POOR LAW

In 1834, a new Poor Law came into being. This was because the Government thought that too much money was being paid to the poor. No outdoor relief was given except for some old and sick people. Everyone else had to enter a workhouse. Many new workhouses were built. These were made as unpleasant as possible. The idea was that people would think twice before asking for help.

Edwin Chadwick.

POOR LAW UNIONS

After 1834, all parishes had to join together forming groups made up of about twenty or thirty of the old parishes. These were known as 'Poor Law Unions'. Together, Unions had more money than single parishes. Each Union could afford to build a workhouse. Some continued to use buildings that had been put up earlier. There was now to be one large, central workhouse for each Union. A Poor Law Department was also set up in London. This was headed by Edwin Chadwick. His job was to be in charge of the Poor Law Unions throughout the country.

THE BOARD OF GUARDIANS

It was decided that life in the workhouse should be more miserable than life for the poorest worker outside. Workhouses became dreadful places. This was meant to stop lazy people from asking for help. Unfortunately there were many people who were unable to work or could not find a job who were forced into the workhouses.

Each Union was run by a group called the 'guardians'. They were elected by the local ratepayers.

The board of guardians supervised and chose the staff to run the workhouse. People asking for relief were interviewed by the board. The woman in the picture is weak from hunger. She has fainted in front of the guardians.

A woman faints before the guardians.

THE "MILK" OF POOR-LAW "KINDNESS."

A woman is separated from her child in the workhouse, 1843.

THE CRUEL NEW LAW

The new workhouses were hated. Wives were now separated from husbands, children from parents, brothers from sisters. They were usually kept apart in different dormitories, where they slept, and different yards, where they exercised. This splitting up of families was thought by many to be the worst part of the new Poor Law. Sometimes infants were allowed to be kept by their mothers until they were old enough to be sent to lessons. Sadly though, this did not always happen.

The picture shows a mother having her child dragged from her by the workhouse matron. In the background, the devil smiles while an angel weeps. Do you think the person who drew this was for or against workhouses?

THE EXERCISE YARD

This picture shows the women's yard of a Union workhouse in the 1840s. Many of those who ended up in the workhouse were young children, the old and the sick. The deaf old lady on the left is using an ear trumpet to listen to the person next to her. They are all wearing workhouse uniform. There is washing on the line. This was one of the jobs women had to do. The letters V.R. on the wall are short for Victoria *Regina* – Latin for Queen Victoria.

Women gather in the laundry yard.

WORKHOUSE UNIFORM

When paupers entered the workhouse, they had to hand over their own clothes, and put on a uniform. These were of plain appearance. They would have been worn by a lot of other people. Many disliked this. They felt they were being treated like criminals going into a prison.

The wooden dolls in the picture are dressed in uniforms similar to those worn by people in the workhouse. The dolls' clothes are made with scraps from material that was used for workhouse uniforms. They were made by the poor of Thursford Workhouse in Norfolk between 1898 and 1900.

Workhouse dolls.

Attack on Stockport workhouse, 1842.

MARCHES AND DEMONSTRATIONS

Workhouses were very unpopular throughout the country. In some areas, there were marches and demonstrations against them. The biggest opposition to the new Poor Law came from the northern industrial towns. People in the north suffered from dreadful poverty and were desperate about the conditions they lived in. In Stockport, a group of the townspeople broke into the workhouse and stole food and clothing. In the picture, you can see some of them holding up the bread they have taken.

Rules and REGULATIONS

The new Poor Law said there should be very strict rules in workhouses. These had to be the same in all workhouses. The rules included such things as what could be eaten at meals and what time to go to bed. There were also rules about behaviour, doing chores and keeping clean.

OLIVER TWIST

This is a picture taken from *Oliver Twist*, a novel by Charles Dickens. In this book, Dickens describes what it was like to be an orphan brought up in a workhouse. For example, there is a description of the food the children ate. The workhouse, Dickens says, gave three meals of thin gruel a day. Gruel is a porridge made mainly with water and a tiny amount of oatmeal. Oliver was still hungry when he finished his gruel, and he went and asked for more.

'Please, sir, I want some more.'

THE DIETARY SHEET

Food in workhouses was very dull. It was a little better, though, than the meals described in *Oliver Twist*. There were instructions about the weight and type of food that could be provided. You can see this on the dietary sheet of the Mitford and Launditch Union. This was printed in the mid-nineteenth century for the workhouse at Gressenhall in Norfolk. Other workhouses had similar rules. As well as gruel, for example, the paupers were given bread and cheese and, sometimes, a meat or suet pudding. Women and children received smaller amounts of the same things given to men.

PUNISHMENT

The workhouse master was often very strict. Paupers who broke any of the rules were punished. Their names were put in the punishment book. Those who talked at meal times or used bad language, for example, were called 'disorderly' as were those who refused to work. Disorderly paupers were fed on bread and water for two days. Those who broke the rules again within a week, or were rude to anyone in charge, were called 'refractory' (this means being obstinate, and not learning one's lesson). Paupers could be punished by being put in a room by themselves for up to twenty-four hours. This room might have no light, and was often like a cell. No wonder workhouses became known as the new prisons.

DIETARY FOR ABLE BODIED PAUPERS OF BOTH SEXES.		BREAKFAST.		DINNER.						SUPPER.	
		Bread.	Gruel.	Suet Pudding with Vegetables.	Bread.	Cheese.	Butter.	Meat Pudding with Vegetables.	Broth.	Bread.	Cheese.
		oz.	Pints.	oz.	oz.	oz.	oz.	oz.	Pints.	oz.	oz.
SUNDAY.	Men	7	1½	-	-	-	-	14	-	7	1
	Women	6	1½	-	-	-	-	12	-	6	½
MONDAY.	Men	7	1½	-	7	-	-	-	1½	7	1
	Women	6	1½	-	6	-	-	-	1	6	¾
TUESDAY.	Men	7	1½	-	7	1	-	-	-	7	1
	Women	6	1½	-	6	¾	-	-	-	6	¾
WEDNESDAY.	Men	7	1½	-	7	1	-	-	-	7	1
	Women	6	1½	-	6	¾	-	-	-	6	¾
THURSDAY.	Men	7	1½	14	-	-	-	-	-	7	1
	Women	6	1½	12	-	-	-	-	-	6	¾
FRIDAY.	Men	7	1½	-	7	1	-	-	-	7	1
	Women	6	1½	-	6	¾	-	-	-	6	¾
SATURDAY.	Men	7	1½	-	7	1	-	-	-	7	1
	Women	6	1½	-	6	¾	-	-	-	6	¾

The diet sheet of the Mitford and Launditch Union.

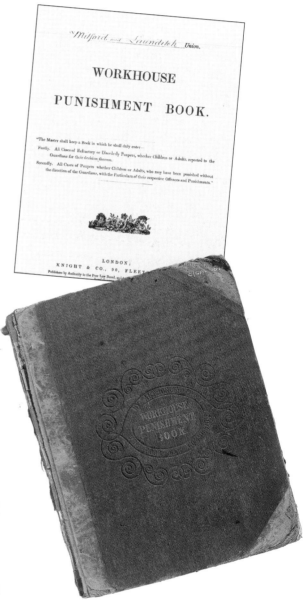

The workhouse punishment book.

PICKING OAKUM

The oakum shed at Coldbath Fields Prison.

Some of the jobs done in workhouses, such as breaking stones and oakum picking, were the same as those done by prisoners. Oakum was rope covered in tar. It was used to fill the cracks on wooden ships to make them watertight. When it needed replacing, the oakum was sent to workhouses and prisons. The paupers or prisoners then had the job of unravelling and removing the tar from the rope. An iron hook or spike was used to help. It was still very hard on the fingers. Oakum picking was one of the most hated jobs in the workhouse.

EDUCATION AND TRAINING

There was a more positive side to life in workhouses. Some workhouses tried to train adults to do something useful, like learning a trade. They could, for example, learn tailoring or shoe-making. It was hoped that one day they might be able to support themselves outside the workhouse.

Children, also, were often given a good, basic education. They were taught reading, writing and arithmetic. This was something many children outside the workhouse did not get until the Education Act of 1870 provided state education for all.

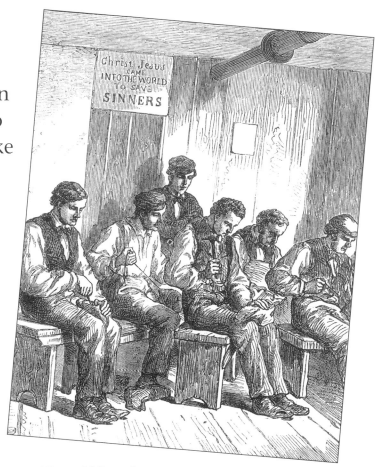

The cobbling class.

Nutmeg grater seller.

STREET SELLERS

Workhouses still remained places that were dreaded by the poor. Many preferred to take their chances on the streets. There were lots of street sellers in the nineteenth century. The picture shows one of these sellers. This crippled man is trying to scrape a living by selling nutmeg graters. For him, life would not have been easy. In difficult times he, too, would have to ask for poor relief.

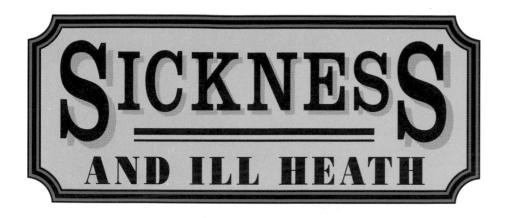

SICKNESS
AND ILL HEATH

Illness was one of the main causes of poverty in Victorian times. Ill health and early death were much more common than they are in Britain today. There were many dangerous diseases. This was a big problem in the overcrowded new towns. These towns grew quickly at the beginning of the nineteenth century, especially those in the north of England.

OVERCROWDED TOWNS

Victorian towns were a maze of alleys and courtyards. You can see in this picture the heaps of rotting garbage that were dumped in narrow streets. Children played on these piles of rubbish. Others dug through the refuse, hoping to find something of use or value. It would have been smelly and very unhealthy.

Very poor people came to the towns from the countryside looking for work in one of the new factories. They lived in cramped lodging houses that were rented as temporary homes for travellers. Able-bodied men sometimes left their families in the workhouse while they tried to find a job.

A dirty street in 1852.

A LONDON STREET

This scene shows a street with people at every window and doorway. Houses like these had to be shared. Whole families were crowded into single rooms which would have been very cramped. Perhaps that is why so many children were out in the street late at night. The very poor lived in cellars. These were dark and damp. There were no windows and very little air. There was also a lack of piped water and drains. Disease could spread quickly in places like this. Many were made paupers by illness because they were unable to work.

Dudley Street, London by Gustav Dore.

Robert Owen.

FACTORY OWNERS

Many town houses were put up by the factory owners. They were built quickly and cheaply. Most employers did not care about their workers. The workers were not paid much and they had to live in slums. There were a few factory owners who were not greedy or cruel. Robert Owen was one of these. He wanted to improve the lives of his workers. He thought they should be treated well.

A CURE FOR POVERTY

Owen's factory at New Lanark in Scotland.

Robert Owen ran a cotton factory at New Lanark in Scotland. He believed that he could make a profit and still treat his workers well. He reduced the normal working hours of his workers, and raised their wages. He also provided good housing and schooling. A shop was opened to sell goods at fair prices. Each week he took some money from the workers' wages for a special fund. This was used to pay his workers when they fell sick or became too old to work. Few, sadly, followed Owen's example. The poor who were sick elsewhere often ended up in the workhouse.

KING CHOLERA

For most people living in towns, disease and poverty were common. Some diseases were spread by filthy drinking water. One of the most dreaded was cholera. It spread easily in unclean water and many people died from it. The disease was so powerful that some called it King Cholera. The lack of pure water was a serious problem. There was usually one stand-pipe for the street. It was turned on for about an hour or two a day. Most town water was pumped, untreated, from the nearest river. The poor had to fill up buckets and pans. Even if it seemed clean, the water was rarely fit to drink.

Collecting water.

BACK TO THE WORKHOUSE

It was not surprising that many of the poor fell ill. People could be made paupers when disease threw one of the family out of work. Gradually, however, conditions in the workhouses did begin to get better. Rules became less strict, although uniforms still had to be worn and families remained separated from one another. In the picture you can see that the women were not allowed to eat with the men, or with the children. As time passed, the food improved but, despite this and other changes for the better, workhouses remained places feared by the poor.

Dinner time at St Pancras workhouse, London, 1895.

WORKHOUSE ALTERNATIVES

Not all poor people ended up in the workhouse. Most poor people hated the idea of going to such a place. Some preferred to starve than put up with the treatment they would receive in a workhouse. Others tried begging or turned to crime. In towns, the number of homeless people grew. Those wanting to lead honest lives, without asking for relief, found it more and more difficult to do so.

TRADE UNIONS

One way that the poor could try to improve things was by joining a trade union. A trade union is a group of workers who come together to campaign for better working conditions and better wages. Such groups, to begin with, had little success because the workers were in fear of losing their jobs. In this picture, farm labourers are meeting in secret, and at night. They wanted to avoid the watchful eye of the farmer who employed them.

A meeting of an agricultural labourers' union.

LABOUR YARDS

In some towns, labour yards were set up, like this one at Bethnal Green in London. The labour yard was a place where men worked in return for food, but, unlike a workhouse, they did not have a bed to sleep there. The men in this yard are breaking stones which were used for making roads. You can see that they are wearing goggles to protect their eyes from flying shrapnel. The job of stone-breaking was also done in the workhouses.

Stone-breaking in a labour yard.

EMIGRATION

Some people tried to avoid poverty and unemployment by emigrating. This meant starting a new life in another country. Emigration Committees were set up in many places in Britain to help and encourage the poor to go to places such as Canada, Australia and New Zealand. Emigrating was not an easy thing to do. Friends and family were left behind. A long and dangerous sea voyage was involved, spending weeks aboard overcrowded ships. Although some emigrants died on the journey, many people were willing to take the risk in the hope of starting a better life abroad. For them, life at home had nothing to offer.

Scottish emigrants set sail for Canada.

HERE AND THERE

In Britain, many parishes found it cheaper to pay their unemployed the fare to another country than to keep them at home. This is because there would then be fewer paupers in the workhouses to be kept by the parish at the ratepayers' expense.

To persuade people to go overseas, there were many advertisements that showed how life abroad could be much better than at home. People were attracted by the way of life away from Britain's crowded cities. Not everyone was successful abroad. Some people were lucky and found work in the new country and succeeded in buying some land and building themselves a home. However, many others were less fortunate and died in poverty.

The advantages of emigration.

HERE AND THERE;

SOUP KITCHENS

Many of the poor were not willing to leave their homeland. Life might have been hard in this country, but they were not prepared to take a chance elsewhere. At times of particular hardship, the local church sometimes organized relief. Soup kitchens were common in Victorian Britain. In the picture on page 27, the room is filled with the poor who would not enter a workhouse. Each person was given a bowl of soup.

THE LOCAL SCHOOL

Helping the hungry, 1867.

Conditions became a little better in workhouses as the years passed by. There was better treatment for the sick. Life was made easier for the aged poor. Paupers were sometimes allowed visitors in the workhouse and trips outside. After the education reforms of 1870, pauper children were often educated in the local state schools. In this photograph, you can identify the workhouse boys from their shaven heads and uniforms. By the end of Victoria's reign, workhouses remained places that the needy only turned to if there was no alternative.

Children from Gressenhall workhouse in Norfolk attend the local school.

TIME LINE

BC AD 0		500	
	43	410	
		'THE DARK AGES'	
CELTS	ROMAN BRITAIN	ANGLO-SAXONS	VIKINGS

EARLY 1800s

1815 The Corn Laws keep the price of bread high.

1819 Queen Victoria born.

1825 End of the Combination Acts makes trade unions legal.

1830s

1830 Farm labourers burn ricks and destroy machines in southern England.

1832 Outbreak of cholera. Many thousands die.

1834 New poor law begun by the Poor Law Amendment Act.

1837 Queen Victoria's reign begins.

1838 Charles Dickens writes *Oliver Twist*.

1840s

1842 Edwin Chadwick publishes a report which shows disease is spread by overcrowding and lack of pure water.

1846 End of the Corn Laws.

1848 Cholera breaks out again, and over 70,000 people die.

1850s

1852 First public lavatories in London.

1854 Florence Nightingale introduces big improvements into nursing during the Crimean War, and her ideas soon spread in Britain.

| 1066 | | 1485 | 1603 | 1714 | 1837 | 1901 |

MIDDLE AGES

NORMANS TUDORS STUARTS GEORGIANS VICTORIANS 20TH CENTURY

1860s

1866 First Barnardo home for destitute children opened in Stepney.

1866 Between 18,000 and 20,000 people die from cholera.

1870s

1870 Forster's Elementary Education Act makes schooling compulsory for most children.

1872 Joseph Arch's Agricultural Labourers' Union tries to organize farm workers so that they can improve their wages.

1875 Artisans' Dwellings Act tries to deal with overcrowding in towns by clearing slum areas and re-housing people.

1876 Dr. Barnardo estimates that about 30,000 children sleep rough in London.

1880s

1884 Reform Act gives the vote to farm workers.

1887 Queen Victoria's Golden Jubilee.

1890s

1897 Queen Victoria's Diamond Jubilee.

1900s

1901 Death of Queen Victoria.

1908 Old Age Pensions started for those over 70 years old.

1911 National Health Insurance started. In return for weekly contributions when they are working, wage-earners receive payment if they fall sick.

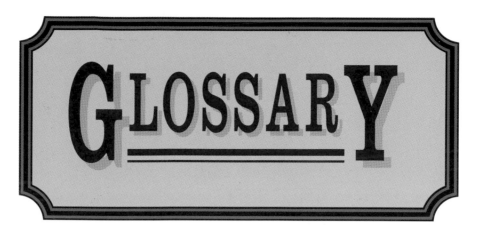

GLOSSARY

Able-bodied poor The poor people who were thought to be fit and capable of working.

Apprentice A child who worked for a master, and learnt how to do a job, in return for food, clothes and shelter.

Charity Help given to poor, sick and helpless people.

Cholera A disease that was carried in unclean water, and led to choking, vomiting, black blotches on the skin and, often, death.

Emigration To leave one's own country to live in another country.

Eviction Forcing a family from their home.

Gruel A mixture of oatmeal in milk or water.

Guardian One who takes care of someone or something.

Labourer A worker who does not need special training to do his job.

Oakum Loose fibre obtained by picking old rope to pieces.

Orphan A child with no parents.

Overseer of the Poor Someone who used to look after poor and sick people.

Parish A division of the country that has its own church.

Pauper A very poor person.

Poacher Someone who steals wild animals, including birds and fish, from someone else's land.

Poor laws Laws to do with the way that poor people who could not support themselves were given shelter and food.

Poor rate A tax paid by people with money to help the poor.

Poor relief Help given to the poor, such as food, money or shelter.

Poverty The condition of being poor.

Reform To alter and improve something.

Slums Overcrowded houses, often without drains or water supply.

Soup kitchen A place where food and drink, especially soup, is served to the poor.

Union A joining together of things into one.

BOOKS TO READ

Bainbridge, J. *People* (Basil Blackwell, 1980)
Harper, R. *Finding Out About Victorian Childhood* (Batsford, 1986)
Jamieson, A. *The Industrial Revolution* (Edward Arnold, 1982)
Ross, S. *Spotlight on the Victorians* (Wayland, 1988)
Sauvain, P. *A Victorian Factory Town* (Macmillan, 1982)
Styles, S. *The Poor Law* (Macmillan, 1985)
Triggs, T. *Victorian Britain* (Wayland, 1990)

PLACES TO VISIT

The following museums have displays and exhibitions to do with social history.

ENGLAND

Avon: Empire and Commonwealth Museum, Clock Tower Yard, Temple Meads, Bristol, BS1 6QH. Tel. 0272 254983
Dorset: The Old Crown Court, High Street West, Dorchester, DT1 1UZ. Tel. 0308 22116
Gloucestershire: Cirencester Lock-Up, Trinity Road, Cirencester, GL7 1BR. Tel. 0285 655611
Cotswold Countryside Collection, Northleach, Gloucester, GL54 3JH. Tel: 0451 60715
Kent: Dickens House Museum, 2 Victoria Parade, Broadstairs, CT10 1QS. Tel. 0843 62853
Manchester: National Museum of Labour History, 103 Princess Street, Manchester, M1 6DD. Tel. 061 2287212
Norfolk: Rural Life Museum, Gressenhall, Dereham, NR20 4DR. Tel. 0362 860563
West Yorkshire: Dewsbury Museum, Crow Nest Park, Dewsbury, WF13 2SA. Tel. 0924 468171

SCOTLAND

Lanark: New Lanark Mills, Lanark, ML11 9DB. Tel. 0555 61345
Lothian: The People's Story, Canongate Tolbooth, 163 Canongate, Edinburgh, EH8 8BN. Tel. 031 2252424
Scottish Agricultural Museum, Ingliston, Edinburgh, EH2 1JD. Tel. 031 3332674

Strathclyde: Summerlee Heritage Trust, West Canal Street, Coatbridge, ML5 1QD. Tel. 0236 440429

WALES

Glamorgan: Welsh Folk Museum, St. Fagans, Cardiff, CF5 6XB. Tel. 0222 569441
Gwynedd: Beaumaris Gaol and Courthouse, Beaumaris, Anglesey. Tel. 0248 810921

NORTHERN IRELAND

County Tyrone: Ulster American Folk Park, Mellon Road, Castletown, Omagh, BT78 5QY. Tel: 0622 243292

INDEX